Outside the Fold,
Outside the Frame

Outside the Fold,
Outside the Frame

Anita Skeen

For Mary Ellen —
Ghost Ranch is truly
a magic place where
magic things happen —
like our workshop. Thanks
for making it magic, and
I hope I'll see you next
summer.
Fondly,
Anita
4 Aug. 2000

Michigan State University Press
East Lansing

∞ The paper used in this publication meets the minimum require-
ments of ANSI/NISO Z39.48-1992 (R 1997) (Permanence of Paper).

Michigan State University Press
East Lansing, Michigan 48823-5202

03 02 01 00 99   1 2 3 4 5

Library of Congress Cataloging-in-Publication Data

Skeen, Anita.
   Outside the fold, outside the frame / Anita Skeen.
   p. cm.
   ISBN 0–87013–512–0 (alk. paper)
   1. Women—Poetry. I. Title.
   PS3569.K374 O98 1999   99-6068
   811'.54—dc21   CIP

Cover Design by Heidi Dailey
Book Design by Michael J. Brooks
Cover Artwork by Tess Marie Johnson

Visit Michigan State University Press on the World-Wide Web
www.msu.edu/unit/msupress

for the women who came before me,
and will come after, whose lives have gone
unnoticed and whose voices remain unheard

Contents

III. THE INNER CITY OF DREAMS

IV. A THIRD EYE

Acknowledgments

Some of the poems in this volume were originally published in the following places:

a Sense of Place, *The Smith*
Last Night October, This Morning November, *Mid America Review*
The Artist Travels the Kansas Turnpike, Wichita to Topeka, On Valentine's Day, *Kansas Quarterly*
The Professor Maps Her After Hours Itinerary, *The Midland Review*
The Muse Speaks in Four Voices, *The Poetry Miscellany*
Baptist Hymns, *The Atlanta Review*
Fixing the Moon, *Prairie Schooner*
Elizabeth Responds to the Separation, *My Lover is a Woman* (Ballantine Books)
The English Teacher, in Mid-Life, *Worlds in Our Words: Contemporary American Women Writers* (Prentice Hall)
Taking Down the Tree, *There's No Place Like Home for the Holidays* (Papier Mache)
The Woman Whose Body is Not Her Own, *I Am Becoming the Woman I Always Wanted*, (Papier Mache)

I would like to express my appreciation to the MacDowell Colony and the Virginia Center for the Creative Arts for providing me with both the time and the place to complete this manuscript.

I have a theory that every time you make an important choice, the part of you left behind continues the other life you could have had. . . . There's a chance that I'm not here at all, that all the parts of me, running along all the choices I did and didn't make, for a moment brush against each other. . . . I have not gone forward or back in time, but across time, to something I might have been, playing itself out.

Jeanette Winterson
Oranges Are Not The Only Fruit

I. House of Cards

Raven Tells a Story

At dusk, the ravens come to call.
They taxi singly and in pairs
to the attics of cedar and fir,

the straight-back pines. *(Something's
up*, say their trickster grins.
We know, we know, they crow.)

There's discord in the ranks, much
raucous complaint. The ducks
on the island bark back,

quacks tangled and sharp.
Much flapping of wings, in water,
in air, agitation of fowl

and then your call:

I would like to write the words
flowed between us like the hushed
water of this lake, highway

of duck and heron, conduit for bass
and shimmering trout, even murky safety
for the occasional startled frog.

But tonight the winds are up
(the ravens know) and words surge
through the phone wires

in tidal waves. You cannot hear
what I say. Like Xerxes,
I think I can turn back the sea.

Like Xerxes, I fail.
(Raven begins the tale:
Long ago, a woman came to the shore

of Silver Lake. She cut logs. . .
We both ride out the storm
grabbing chair and table,

bedpost and chest, look for
anchors in shared space. . . .
and then, a stranger

came with a letter. . .)
In the wreckage of words
we surrender.

I won't throw the last stone.
You can't walk away, slam the door.
But I give in, then cradle

the receiver like an old bone,
sacred tool, ceremonial
pipe put to rest.

(The two were happy, until,
unexpectedly. . . . Raven drops
a sable feather from her wing.)

The house is dark.
I've turned on no lamps.
I look out to the lake

where lips of water kiss
the jagged rocks, without pain,
their murmurings a story

I eavesdrop on each night.
Tonight the clatter of ravens,
insistent and scornful, denies them.

(This is the way it was
in the time of First Bird.
This is the way it is, even now.)

Outside, I search for the cause
of such chaos. The branches are dark,
feathered in accusation.

There is no moon to promise me light.

First Learning

I remember that moment because
I planned, at six in the first grade,
to remember the moment forever.
                    —Donald Hall

Smell, they say, is the corridor, the passage
back through laundry and the mortgage,
the rabbit hole to Wonderland:
the first grade classroom, late afternoon
light drowsing around twenty children locked behind
green readers, and I walk in,
the new kid, in early April, friendships
and hatreds already lifetimes old,
escorted by Mrs. Sippe, the principal,
who tells my name and forces the small voices
to give it back in chorus,
but it is the smell of old wood worn
slick I respond to, the chalk rail
and desks, the floorboards and doorframes,
the cloakroom odor of lunchbox lids
just lifted, and bodies too warm
in their woollen leggings. I smell hands
dirty and blistered from the monkeybars,
the cache of fireballs confiscated to the trash.
In this permanent moment I am filed
in a desk with the S's while forty wide eyes
decide who I really am. Mrs. Overfield,
my now first grade teacher, hands me
a slick white paper, limp and purple-inked,
with words and shapes I know
I must know. I lift the page to my face,
sniff the damp sweetness of mimeo,

the whiff which will forever mean *stranger,*
the triangle which I see instantly
does not belong in Row A
with those four-sided perfect squares.

Dustrags

The worn flannel rips easily, fast
as a zipper. If I start the tear,
it almost takes off by itself.
Last night, my clenched fist
went through the right shoulder
as I tugged it over my head.
The cloth's too old to sew.
Nothing but shreds, nothing
to loop the thread through.

Nine pieces now. When the boys
wash cars, polish chrome, what
will they know about the cloth,
soft as a cow's nose? This nightgown,
brown squares printed in slightly
crooked rows, goes back
farther than their past.
What do you save this for? they ask.

My mother taught me: throw
nothing away. A plastic jug
makes a garden marker, grocery
sacks convert to Halloween masks,
wrapping paper has an afterlife.
I wipe the teak desk with the sleeve
of a gown I wore before you
left, wash windows with a stitched hem,
scrub the claw-footed tub
with a front placket, buttons
carefully clipped off and kept
in a biscuit tin.

Elegy on a Summer Night

Tonight, cooking ears of sweet corn,
I remember my grandmother
at family gatherings, sharp knife
in hand, shaving her corn
from the cob in neat planks,
leaving it planed like a 2 x 4
because she had false teeth.
All the cousins looked on in awe
as she mixed the yellow slabs
with her half runner beans
and devoured the lot.
Do mine like that! we cried,
elbowing close to her plate,
Me first!

Tonight on the phone my mother,
a continent away, tells me my uncle,
three states north of her,
is hospitalized in a coma.
I will not remember him like this
but in the dewy light
of West Virginia summer mornings,
how he arrives with buckets
of chubby peaches and bushel baskets
of beans, a carload of melons
and a wild Hawaiian shirt.
He drops down the tailgate.
Cousins spill from the red wagon.

It's his heart again, she says.
It's been going for years.
He's not the first to go.
My uncle in Phoenix with bad lungs.
And years before, my grandmother,
cancer flowering in her brain.

It's July once again.
I'm alone in a cabin on a lake.
Families camp in a park nearby.
I smell dinners cooking: woodsmoke
and burgers, charcoal and chicken.

I think of those ritual summer
picnics, relatives plentiful
as fresh corn, the cousins outside
for hours orbiting in the dark
till ground control called us in,
lightning bugs blinking the path home.

Tonight some of these cousins
take planes, drive cars
to the North Carolina coast,
come in to their father
for the last time.
I am nearly the age
of my grandmother
when she stood in that small
kitchen wearing housedress
and apron, sawing at the corn,
surprising us with the ordinary
like she did all her life.

Tonight, as I watch the ducks
taxi in toward their soft island
nests and darkness suck light
from the firs, I think of the cousins
scattered random as these stars—
California, Colorado, Michigan,
Oklahoma, Texas, Arizona
Florida, North Carolina, Alaska—
each of us losing, from the constellation
of memory, one more fixed body
as my uncle's light fades,
each of us burning a little
less bright.

Disappearing Acts

Last night, on my way to the kitchen,
I noticed the painting of two beagles,
hanging for years in the hall, was missing
(not unlike the beagles themselves):
the wall white, the space blank, the hook
slightly tilted to the right, the picture
gone. This morning the money I keep
in a blue Guatemalan pouch beneath
the bathroom sink has disappeared.
Lysol, the sewing kit, the small electric
heater and political buttons—Pat Schroeder
for President, Geraldine Ferraro, George
McGovern (lost causes all)—smile
victoriously from the basket. But the money,
unspent and unreal Canadian bills, is gone.
Just now, the boy in the Notre Dame cap
two seats in front of me on the train
cannot find his ticket. He searches
luggage, pockets, trash sacks, the fold-up
table on the back of the seat. The ticket
agent scoffs, suggesting impossible possibilities.
The couples across the aisle talk of
the game Notre Dame lost to Florida State.
You've lost your mind, the husband tells
the wife, waving his glasses to make the point.
We've lost the trees, I remember saying
to my mother last August when we cut down
seven, each bare as a wish bone,
Dutch elm disease raiding the neighborhood.
I think about my mother, who for months
has been searching for a lost album, photos
of my grandfather, lost to drowning,
and my grandmother, lost to cancer,
lost now, it seems, forever.
All these vacancies around us, the world
vanishing piece by random piece.

After She Left

and I want to ask you
here, in the sterile lobby
of this drafty theater,

what did you do when she left you,
long before she left the marriage?
What did the silence in the house mean?

Or that you and the cat shared the bed?
I heard you had your bags packed too.
Did you ever ask her back

or do you ever want to?
What do you feel when you pass
my house, hear my name in the room?

Instead, I ask if you will leave town
next September, and you say
you like my new haircut, have never seen me

in glasses before. I touch your arm
with whimsical advice, playing
old friend, feel the seam

of your undershirt beneath your sleeve.
A strange intimacy, it seems,
here in this place crowded as memory,

no one else knowing
how the lines of our lives cross,
why we pause now, honoring connection.

Tattoo

It was the color
that drew me

not the filagree
of your name

or the suggestion
dormant under cotton

under silk.
And the pain:

memory of the needle
a steel sorrow

burrowing in my skin
grief pushing

through flesh.
The heart

does not need a tattoo.
It refuses the visible:

the cerulean, the torch
red loops and curls, indelible

coils, the filament
of yellow,

the letters mute
the story tucked in.

Last Night October, This Morning November

Morning begins with the invasion
of geese, squadron after squadron, coming
in from the north, circling, making contact,
their radio frequencies haywire, static
all over the sky. The dog and I go out
to our narrow deck, watch them gather
overhead like seeds for a funnel
cloud, then some scatter
in the sky's furrows
while others splash down
on the lake like stones. They
remain throughout the day and tonight,
after it all, their insisting presence
shrinks the darkness to the curve
of their black necks.

My oldest friend, of forty-four years, turns
fifty today, only a month after I have.
When we both turned thirty, I wrote her
a poem, a favorite still. I think of writing
For Susan, Turning Fifty, think how that final word
is wrong, how it should be omitted, how the focus
should be on the word before, the turning.
For Susan, Turning. Twenty years after
that first poem, I see there is no
finality, that we are never anything
more than a moment, and then, we are
something else. I think of the geese I watched this morning
turning overhead, banking, the V of their flight
in disarray, shards of the vector thumping
against the lake, winged squawks turning into
feathered boats, bodies in air, just like that,
bodies at sea

~ ~ ~

Another friend, my oldest in town, calls to say
her dog is dying. We've known this a long time,
but today, there's no denying. These are the last
hours she knows. The time in the future is now.
I meet her at the vet's where this is confirmed.
For one brief moment she has the chance to sweep
the dog from the Formica table into the marshmallow
sleeves of her winter parka, to turn and leave
the room, flecked body breathing against
her chest. There is that moment, then it's past,
and we are headed into another life, all of us,
the dog leaping from her limp body
into a brightness we can only imagine
as her head settles, after the injection,
into the crook of my arm. How thick the darkness
under such invasive lights, thick with memory,
thick as pond water.

~ ~ ~

Driving home, I think there are tears
on the windshield, barely visible, not like
my own, when I realize they are snowflakes,
the first of the season. They turn
to water when they hit the warm glass.
This will not be a deep snow, only
its foreshadowing. I think how
for nearly fifty years there has been
a first snow, a first flake, recognition
striking like flint, and I feel the turning
of fall into winter, the way we will hunker
down in our homes through this season of short days
and long dark, the way we have already begun
waiting for spring. I turn from Jolly Road

onto Ponderosa, my street, named for tall
dense pines of the west, as a hundred
solid bodies lift from the lake, webbed feet
giving way to frantic wing, rising, turning
south over the roof of my house, turning
into a cloud from which might fall
feathers or snow.

The Woman Whose Body Is Not Her Own

She is not herself anymore,
hasn't been since she stood before the mirror
in her own bathroom, holding
her own toothbrush, an ordinary
gesture, two days
later. She was lucky
to be alive, they all said, lucky
to lose something she didn't need,
not an essential foot
or a necessary hand.
They told her to rest.
They took her to dinner and talked
of the new kittens, the new boss
pestering like a small boy,
the small woman blessing them
from the corner booth.
The women across the table
were intact, might have lost a job
or a tennis match, maybe even
had lost touch with a son
or a good friend.
When she touched what was lost,
splayed her fingers across her chest
like a child cheating a peek
in a nightmare flick,
she heard the word *best*.
This is best, they said.
This is my breast, she tells the woman
in the glass, her hands cupped
like small graves
over the pale landscape, the shadow
of full moons. She feels the lips
of her first baby sucking
at air, sees him nested now in the crook
of his mother's life,
of this other woman's arm.

Between Strangers

I pass through this town, off-the interstate,
to get gas, then see the sign next door
to the Amoco: Jean's Barber Shop.
I park the truck, walk in, never considering
Jean might be a woman, might be Black,
might be someone hesitant to cut
my urchin's mop. She's not sure,
I can tell, but I say *just a shorter version*
of what I have, I can't take the heat,
and she motions toward the chair.
She wraps my neck, hands familiar
as my mother's, her fingers in my hair
tentative and unsure. I'm getting nervous
so I start to talk, find out she's from the city,
lived there all her life till she came
to this small town to get away from bad stuff.
She wants a garden but is afraid of snakes.
She wants to walk but fears the ticks.
We trade more talk as her scissors
snip, split ends and curls drifting
like the early blossoms of flowering trees
now that it's late spring. She snips,
steps back to talk. I watch her hands
draw stories in the air and then she drops
the conversation stopper:
her only son, bleeding to death in that city
from an anonymous shotgun blast,
three months before he was to come
to her. Three years ago. She saw him
in the coffin six months before
it happened, saw him call her
from the top of a haloed stairway
six months later. *Oh no*, she said,
not me. I'm staying here.

16

She prayed her way well.
Now, sometimes, the shop door opens
and closes, and no one comes in.
She touches my head, lifts up
my hair and I imagine that hand reaching
toward the child, the boy, the man,
reaching back to hair she knows
the fabric of, touching the curls
and waves of all her customers, feeling
loss in every one. She says she's better
now, then offers me the mirror to check
her work. Reflected in the glass
to my back I see two women, one in a chair,
the other standing above, like a Victorian
photo, whose lives collide in this room
on a muggy day, both a long way
from home, the air close,
the cutting of hair the farthest thing
from both their minds.

The Quilt: 25 April 1993

It's the hands I see first, on this panel,
the community of hands reaching toward a name
that could be yours, could be mine,
but happens to be Bob's, the hands simple
as those we drew in the primary grades,
tracing around splayed fingers, stubborn thumb,
a ghostly outline on manilla stock.
We cut them out, took them home
to our moms. These hands are fabric,
paisley and denim, tartan and corduroy,
a school of hands swimming toward
Bob's name, hands with their first names
stitched awkwardly in thin thread.
I lay down my own hand, pale one
in the multitude, for enough time
that I feel the hard earth
beneath the weave, a scattering
of small stones. My hand
is the princess resting on the pea.

We move on down the corridor, silent
as those around us. Here's a panel
from Ames, Iowa, one from Kansas, another
from Hawaii, green palm fronds bordering
a blue sea. *This is worse
than the Viet Nam wall*, you say
letting go of your tears. The squares
stretch north and south, east and west,
the four corners of our hearts.
All this color, I think, all this brilliance
about loss. Tom, the next patch says,
then Randy, then Susan.

We say the names aloud, a litany
of stolen light, as we compose
our grief among these postage stamps
of cloth, how we mail our private
and collective message on ahead.

Years Later, Now the Suburbs

In light thin as an old letter
I walk the dog among the shut-tight houses,
windows blank with drawn blinds,
garage doors tight-lipped against asphalt.
They have nothing to reveal.
Husked leaves play on trimmed
lawns prim as cemetery plots.
Only my dog's claws click on the blacktop.
At close of day the world seems closed,
locked up in its autumn skin,
wind zipping shut night's jacket.
In my childhood this was the hour
for blood brothers and promises,
cigarettes in the crawl space,
bright candies traded for things
hushed and forbidden.
The heart of the neighborhood pounded
inside its garb of yard and field.
We perched on the edge
of discovery. We prayed the voices
from the open doors would crack
with someone else's name.
Our secrets flared like struck
matches in the dark.

Short Story

My first time to lunch
with these women whose lives show landscapes
different from my own
and yet, I suspect, teem with the same weathers
all women understand.
I park my truck at Vicki's, who's newly moved
into the home of her dreams.
This house, timbered in wood from forty-eight states,
keeps secrets. In its early time,
scuttling among rockers and trunks, lurked the ghost
of a woman murdered by her spouse,
lately exorcised from the house.
Vicki regrets this now,
imagines a homeless apparition
loose on the east side, wondering
where a ghost goes when finally
deposed. I like her even better
for this concern. Allison, whose voice
I am sure is the voice of God,
if She exists, and Nancy, whose new braces
hiss sibilants like Eve's friend, the snake,
and Linda, the poet, with an apprentice Muse,
haunt the kitchen, clanking ice cubes and spoons.

Over zucchini soup we discuss a local
triple-murder trial and by the time
we're to the strawberries, we all agree
you never know anyone as well as you think,
that we each cultivate places private
as death. But Vicki says, with women friends
she always knows the truth, that she'd learn
in a minute if Linda laced her husband's drink
with Drano. *It's the antennae*, I say,
those electromagnetic waves.

Now we're discussing commencement
addresses and Linda says last night,
at her son's, the speaker was barely
literate. *Be yourself!* he told them
over and over again. Vicki and Allison,
members of the same class twenty-seven years
ago, remember their speaker said, *Make money!*

There's no one within a thousand miles but me
who graduated from Charleston High in 1964,
Climb Every Mountain the theme ringing
through every Senior Class in the country.
And we did. Or I did. These women, too.
We have survived
what we could not imagine then,
at eighteen, planted smiling for the photos
in our pillbox hats and white gloves.
Now, in our forties, we try to imagine
what we could not survive.

Time is running short, I have
to leave, and we all tell Nancy
how she has to write
about her life. I ask if she wants to
write fiction. She says she doesn't know
how. I tell them of the book I fantasized about
as we sat over soup, a novel
opening with five women
forecasting a current murder
trial, and how, as the drama winds out,
so do the statements and cross examination
of each of their own lives.
Write it! says Allison. *Why not
write it today?* And I tell her
I have no feel for plot,
must rely on the impact of the tight image,
the epiphany of language and sound.

Nothing happens in my stories,
I say. *I give you the moment*
which is all.

II. Snipe Hunt

Fixing the Moon

It happened in the night, she said.
She had just passed the upstairs window
on her way to the bathroom and saw it
shimmering in the back yard. She remembered
hearing it hit like a brick, hard and flat.
She thought it was just the neighbor backing
through his garage door again. He always did it
when she was asleep, just for spite.
But then she saw the moon
at a funny tilt like it was just about
to trip on the roof of the Safeway.
She noticed the chunk missing, the bite
out of the bottom. And there it was
in her back yard, burning
like a porch light.

She needed to glue it back before anyone
noticed. Especially the neighbor
who would try to convince the whole street
it was her fault. At K-Mart she asked
for MoonGlue, but the kid with the lisp
who worked in hardware insisted all they had
was Superglue or Elmers. He was sure
they would work. She knew they wouldn't.
Plus, her husband had the extension ladder
at the observatory and wouldn't agree
to bring it back until the weekend, still
four days away. She tried to reach the moon
from the elm in the neighbor's yard.
That was impossible, as she knew it would be.
And the Doberman trying to fly up to the low limbs
didn't help any. She was afraid
that if she didn't put the chunk back soon,
other pieces would chip off like paint.

One was bound to land in the pool when the kids
and five or six friends were splashing about
carefree and unperturbed. They'd be electrocuted,
with her luck, and what would she ever do
with all those bodies?

Eve, Eating Bananas, Sets the Record Straight

It was rumor, that's all.
The press got it wrong . . . again,
didn't check out the source.
But the press was different back then—
mostly prophets and bards
wandering the town spouting off
prediction and history
in verse or psalm. They did love
the language much more,
back then.

It never was an apple.
I should know. I was there.

It was a banana, the pulpy banana
of all knowledge, the banana of longing,
of terminal lust. If we're talking sex
here, and naked flesh, and you're looking
for symbol, which would you
stick in the myth: the chubby apple

or *bananas erectus:*

hard green sleeve, softening,
ripening to yellow, yellow
as the sun, yellow heat,
yellow sin. Peel off the skin,

the unnecessary dress, the cool
limp wrapper of the shaft.
Mold your mouth, sweetly, around
the creamy core, the mushy
lusciousness, and suck shut.
Then snap your teeth

and decapitate. And go at it
again. Open and close,
strip down, swallow mellow.
On the first bite I knew

how to make fire, with the second
I saw the wheel turning through Time,
with the third, the bronze hammer
reverberated in my hand.
By the last bite,

I could write *victim*

in three languages.
All that remained was the peel.
That's what I gave Adam,
who squealed.
By then, I'd had several.
I knew what was coming.
But it was too late.

Or maybe too early.

The press got the story
from the snake who hung coiled
in the tree, that voyeur, that limbless
gland of venom.
He starred himself in the tale,
changing the props,
he said later,
for the sake of Art.
Easier to rhyme *apple*
with *topple* and *fall*,
grapple and *hell*. . .
Try rhyming *banana:*

Havana, cabana, bandanna.
No good for the myth
to end all myths,
the origin of a culture,
the enslavement of a species.
Or a story for children
when they're tucked into sleep,
their curiosity smothered
by parable and cover.

That's how it happened.
Would I lie?

Emily Reveals the Secret of Her Success

1776

I dwell within—my own Desire
That Chamber furnished—Queer
To Others—wayward—uncontrolled
My Vision must appear.

Assembling words—my Housework
I shun the unmade bed
But recipes of Heart—concoct
Such ecstasy! My Bread!

I paint it—natural
Though I tremble at the Sign
Of Death—or God—or stranger's eyes
I never feared—my Mind.

Edna Writes an Odd Sonnet in her Notebook

Once, in the violent months of spring,
I thought that love was everything.
I discovered the light that bronzed the glass
in farmhouse windows I'd casually passed
to be my touchstone, my sensual treasure.
In evening's shades I knew no pleasure
greater than feeling the healing green
glowing from fields where, last month, snow had been.
I'd never imagined, under desperate white,
that April's return would bring such light
whose depth, degree, and fractured slant
could spring my heart's locked-tight regret.
The light splashed in and stained like blood.
I turned in everything to love.

Elizabeth Responds to the Separation

Your absence stirs up frequent conversation
in my brain. I talk to you in rhyme.
I state the facts. I ask for explanation,

my imaginary friend. Silence is aggravation:
winter *sans* snow, the mountain far too steep to climb.
Your absence leads to curious conversation

we would never have at home. Revelation
sprouts in unexpected spots, its bloom sublime.
I state more facts. Your explanation

slips a crocus in my hand. My admiration
escalates. I talk to you (why do they stare?) in mime.
Your absence turns me into conversation

with a cow, a fence. I make a declaration
to the moon at dawn. 0 love! Time
takes her time, that's fact. No explanation

comes for why I miss you so. Infatuation
ages through the years, like wine.
Your absence puts an end to conversation.
I am the fact. You are the explanation.

Duplicate Copy

Inside the suitcase were always two shirts
for every pair of shorts and one additional pair
of underwear, in case anything happened.
That was how my mother packed for summer camp,
vacations, an overnight at a friend's.
You never know, she'd tell me, *you never know
when you'll need a spare.*
So I think all this is really her fault:
there must always be one more jar of mushrooms,
an extra stick of butter, another bottle of ginger ale.
The cupboards have taken over the kitchen:
a calendar above both phones, one on the desk,
another in my billfold, even one on the dishtowel,
all scrawled with identical notes.
There are albums of photos, boxes of reprints,
envelopes with the negatives
in a strongbox and I've just ordered
two copies of a recent best seller plus
a double selection from the Columbia Record Club.
I am concerned about the necessity
to keep duplicate copies of my poems
and xeroxed copies of the duplicates.
I never know what might happen to the originals:
students might steal them, the house could
burn down, consider tornadoes or some other Act of God.
Therefore, things must be located carefully,
logic is important:
one copy on the bookshelf, a second in my office,
a third in my parents' attic,
then the last deposited with an old friend
no one will suspect.
All this must be recorded, of course, and carbons made
in the event the original becomes lost.

My Next Door Neighbor Tells Me Why I Will Have to Work on Monday

You can't depend on blizzards anymore.
You'd think they was made in Taiwan.
All the signs'll be right
and we get nothin' but gray skies.
What good's this cold
without snow
to soften the blows?
Who'd stick up for winter
when all you're gettin' is wind?
Needs somethin' to spit around.
It's like callin' folks to supper and announcin'
No food! Or throwin' a party
and invitin' only the chairs.
Who cares?
Only white around here's my underwear,
and that's not goin' to stop traffic
for three days.
Them storms has got irresponsible as kids,
'bout as absent as breath
in the dead. They tell
you they're comin' the next day
but they never show up.
Just like my cousins.
I find out they went to Harley's
instead, and them responsible for dessert.
Not that the weather's all that on schedule,
but you used to know
there'd be one good blizzard or two.
January. February. It's like they done shot
the groundhog or outlawed sendin' hearts.

They say it's gettin' warmer
everywhere. One day the Alaska water'll be
warm as pig piss. I remember
when it'd come two feet in two days.
School bus wouldn't run.
The 'lectric lines would all come down
and we was in a world of white light.
Now, girl, if you want to stay home,
you better have flu.
Or Uncle Harry pass on.
Don't count on a blizzard.
You'd do better to snipe hunt.

Beaching of the Pilot Whale

for Sally Kitch

It is time. We gather
in deep water like wreckage,
ribs of long ships, ancient
timber. We call to each other,
our voices clear as moonlight,
wind riding the canvas sail.
Our song is not the song
of the mermaids.

Now the sun swims ahead.
We are ready. We slap against
the muscles of the sea, wrestled
down as we swallow the air.
Three miles long, we are a warm
swell seeking the shore.

The sand is cold, but we cannot
rest here. Scores of hands, yapping
like sheep dogs, herd us back
to the shoreline. Weak
from the day's trip
we cannot resist. The sea
collects us one by one, rolls
her woven shawl about us,
takes us home.

It is time. We are fewer
than before. Light appears
above us. We surge
toward the shore.

Riding the Train through Stratford, Ontario Late on
a January Night

The train slows at the town's approach,
lights sudden as fireflies on a summer night.
We bump through the crossing, red signals
beating like a metronome, and I peer
over the strand of double headlights
down the slick street, snow piled high
on either side. The houses hunker dark,
windows looking like old parchment,
scratched with lives: framed painting
above a couch, map pinned over a table,
Tiffany lamp, shadows indecipherable
against a far wall. Next I see The Wild Place

advertising The Brothers Band, glowing
inside like uranium, I know, though the windows
are black and the wooden door a foot thick.
Across the street, The Dominion House, luminous
as snow, its wide picketed porch open to all.
A Budweiser sign hums red and blue neon
in what once must have been a parlor
window, lace curtains flowing behind it.
Town of Lear and MacBeth, Falstaff
and Othello, surely hard drinkers all.
It's The Wild Place I want to walk in,

me drinking a Coke and staring from the train's
false warmth, my double gazing back like Banquo's
ghost. I want to go back tonight
to one dark bar, table top wet with beer
and tears, train whistle blowing
through my heart years before I ever rode
a train. The rocking motion of the room,
the talk of strangers inches from my ear.

The straight line world rumbling by
on its purposeful tracks and me,
tucked into a red vinyl booth,
revolutions of color vibrating
from the juke box, drinking
and traveling nowhere.

Swimming Laps

It's not the last of forty that will do me in,
but these first few, impossibly blue water ahead

for as far as the arm can swim. It must have
looked this way to the good-time folks watching

Noah and his clan bob off like a fat gull on the
rising lake. Or to Crusoe, when he sat beached

looking back, incredulous, at where he had been.
With thirty more to go I'm growing stronger, my

arms forgetting to think what my legs are thinking,
my breath coming in deep heaves. My head scoots

through the water, disembodied, the goof of a young
magician who sawed through the box too soon. At twenty

I'm halfway there, twenty down or twenty left to go,
depending on my philosophical bent, how smooth my stroke,

how rhythmic my kick. The fluid in my body seeks
fluid without, the magnetic pull of the tides each

side of the membrane. My shoreline blurs in the sea's
curving. Ten left to go, I'm like the yacht, slipping

into water like a pale arm into silk. This is the
only skin I've ever worn. Now down to two. The

mermaid and the siren sing, a tune silver as moonlight
on the mirror's wake. My fingers print the slippery

tile as I flip, then my feet, my toes squirming off,
this is the last turn, the final lap, stroke over

stroke, my face in the swell, my body reduced to a
single cell, fearing I will drown when I flounder to air.

Animal Crackers

Speaking with the doctor's receptionist,
I said, *If you can't understand me, it's because*
of the crackers, the animal crackers
I'm chomping right now. She continued,
asked if Monday, March 11, at 9:00 would do
as I bit off the long neck of a giraffe.
My dog was looking hungry, too.
I chose a hippo for her.
We're vegetarian, I added,
but crackers are okay. They aren't real
animals. Or real crackers, for that matter.
I realized she was asking something
about the time.
Yes, I responded, nibbling
the elephant's trunk, *9:00.*

I keep them in the Oreo tin,
I told him, biting off the zebra at the third
stripe. *Up in the window sill.*
The dog hates Oreos, can't stand the creme.
She's getting more and more difficult
to fool. I tell her it's just an eraser,
that lion, or a pebble shaped like a pig.
But she has to sniff it, and that's
that. No more lion. No more pig.
Crunching the camel's hump, I explained:
There are animals now I can't name.
Not that they're strange or exotic.
Nondescript. A fat body, a fat head.
No hoofprints to identify them
left in the cream cheese. No manes
or tails. No horns, pointed
or curled. Why, I wondered, was he
writing all this down?

Not today, I said into the phone.
I'm herding geese. The tigers
have got loose, I stressed, a sheep
in each cheek. *And the dog's no help.*
She's terrified of big cats. She's under
the rocker. That's her howling
right now. I just dropped three on the floor.
Munching four legs at once, I insisted,
Tomorrow's bad, too. It's roundup,
if there's no snow. Time for vitamin A shots,
you know. I'll call if I have trouble,
I promised, gnawing the last panther
in half.

Housebound

My house, I wear
it like a robe, a robe
of many pockets,
many rooms. I am
Joseph in my coat
of many rooms.
To leave, to roam
is to go naked
in the world,
all my private parts
exposed, my body
open to ruin. Out there
I can be sure
of nothing. Here
I am assured. Here
lie my stories,
in rooms: birth
in the blue at the top
of the stairs, death
amid paisley at the end
of the hall. Love
in the kitchen
among vegetables.
Anger in the bedroom
beneath sheets.
My house, my novel,
my plot. Me
in the title role,
my booty surrounding
me. History caught
in a teapot: Great-grandmother
poured from this in
Queen Victoria's reign.

At the Steinway, my religious
life: my soul
ascends on fiery notes,
on wheels of chords.
My house,
where I assemble
myself. I keep my house
close. I plant
my seeds behind drapery
and lamp. The moon
glows in the west after twilight
and in the east before
dawn. Light enters
my many windows. I turn
to see a world constructed
on too large a scale.

My vision
breaks apart: sun
rays collide. A geometry
of fractures, lines,
these pick-up sticks of light,
this house of cards.

Woman Hitchhiking in Niagara Falls

It must've been about 1951. In the picture,
black and white (not color like now), I am too young
for school. I'm gripping a tiny Canadian flag
in my fist. I wear a sailor hat and stand
in front of a stone wall. Somewhere behind me,
out of sight, are the falls. I like to think
the tiny white flecks in the photo are prisms of mist
rising to the sun. That's why I came back,
to see the falls. I thought I'd be able to hear them
from a few miles out of town. Last night,
when the thunder came, I woke fearing the falls.
I got to town at dawn, thought it would be a good time
to see the light's hand-painted tints, see the morning aura
rainbow its way over the water. First I saw
the wax museum, then the Best Buy T-Shirt Shop,
then the million strands of colored beads
cascading through the store windows. The noise
of unfamiliar language was deafening. I saw
a metallic purple car and heard Elvis Presley's voice
moan from inside the next museum. Ads for authentic
plastic moccasins rumbled after me as I started down
the stairs in Queen Victoria Park, careful
not to interfere with the snapshot a Japanese man
was taking of his wife or a woman from Texas
posing her husband. A busload of children
flung a horseshoe around me, arms and legs spilling
from electric neon clothes. I hate to admit it,
but I turned back up the stairs. All I could see
as I looked out was a faint haze, like steam
from the kettle, vaporizing in the air.

Ghost to Pumpkin: A Letter

I see you there, nested in vines
and bedded in leaves, your autumn orange
a solid statement in a vanishing
season. I know about leaves, brilliant
and waxed, that flame like demons
before age warps them to husks
and winds thrash them to dust.
Where are their lights now
in this grey between season?
But there you are, colorfully
napping, sturdy enough to thump on,
plump as an overgrown persimmon,
thoroughly grounded. Do you dream
of a gossamer self, able to slip
from the knotted grasses, able to rise
above your squashed body like steam
from a pot? Do you wonder
what it's like to be fingered
by the wind, to hold the wind, to be
the wind? When you are snatched
from your patch for the carving,
which will happen, will you feel
the knife rip your tight-lipped skin?
Is this the source of hollow sound?
Eyes, nose, teeth that would be
an orthodontist's delight: you become
the carver's worst fear, the hostess'
clever art, the child's lantern.
Light will glow in your belly,
fire dance in your eyes.

How I would like to hold your warmth,
your burning, your flame
that for a moment transforms
such ordinary night: horsemen clatter
along the boards of memory, the moon
ducks behind whipped clouds,
pie-round and smiling.

Variations on the Number 9

There, on the far side, my Achilles pin,
single survivor of the Domino Effect,
wobbling the tick tock of a metronome.
Nine pins in every frame do not add up
to ten points less than a perfect game,
but a 90, a nothing, a nine and an oh.

       In the ball game, it's the bottom of the ninth,
       my team's behind 1-0, 3 on the bases, and I
       strike out.

       I was born in the ninth month
       and at the age of 6, turned my life
       upside down. I traveled Route 66
       through 9 states. Nine numbers appear
       on my social security card, a new math
       kind of name, the final syllable a 9.

I aim the ball down the lane
and it zings by, millimeters from
the traitor pin, a misfire by the firing
squad. A Beethoven symphony crashes
in my brain. The next time
I throw the ball only two pins remain
and on my second try I score
a direct hit. The duo thump down:
but a phantom pin appears behind them,
a ghost pin, a white exclamation point
at the sentence's end. Nine pins,
again. I swear they have 9 lives.

I remember Sunday mornings in Mr. Sirbaugh's
rowdy 4th grade class singing about the ninety
and nine that safely lay in the shelter of the fold
while the shepherd searched through the night
for the one lost. I knew even then I was
that one outside the fold, outside
the frame, the lost lamb, the last pin,
the one keeping the story
from the perfect score.

III. The Inner City of Dreams

The Muse Speaks in Four Voices

Fire

I am language: splinter
and spark. Witches know
what I say, how

to listen, how to put their ears
to my light, how to move

in and out with my tide.
You must study the moon.

I am the link, the trigger,
the thorn. Hurry:

there is no time
to waste, to seek refuge
or sleep. I am known by the bark

I burn, what I take
for my own. I am ash,

memory.

Snow

I am the present tense,
now. I choose not to remember.
Or give the future

in my milk glass globe.
I am the opening to darkness,
darkness reflected off stars, proof
of the power of sunlight.

I am the leopard
wrapped around the earth,
the junco in rush beds. So white
I am blue. I will teach you
to say goodbye, to say

ending.

Mountain

I am the earth's heart pushing,
looking for a way out. I beat
toward the sun. I sharpen

myself on rock, hibernate
inside pine. Myth

hangs in my caves
like bats. Bones tell me
how far I have come.

Raccoon, bear, deer, rabbit:
you stalk me if you hunt
their tracks. My word

is petroglyph. I am
an unfinished chapter, I am

meaning.

Stream

I am a beam, a trail
of light swimming among ferns.
My channel is deeper

than it appears. I slice clean
through stone. If you touch me
you touch the axe blade, you touch

yourself, liquid and cold.
I am distortion

of all you are sure
you know. I do not follow

logic. I do not distinguish
truth from lie. I am what is real,

your story.

The Printer Considers Her Artistic Heritage

In her dotage, my great-grandmother
took up needlepoint, planting tiny roses
on the footstools, potting bouquets
of violets in dainty frames
on the wallpapered hall.
Her stitches seemed fractions
of fractions, 1000 petals
in the needle's eye.

My grandmother discovered crochet,
eggshell thread spinning webs
thicker than spiders' nets,
intricate as Queen Anne's Lace.
Crosses for bookmarks,
tiny doilies studded with dime
store pearls, a hat like a quilted
lid I wore through the winters of childhood.

And my mother, retiring in Florida,
turned to the sea's leavings,
filling her home with mollusk
and conch. Cochinas perch
like butterflies on the lid
of a clamshell candy dish.
Angel wings, abalone, and sand
dollar she tools into necklace
and bracelet, pendant and pin,
her house a walk-in jewelry box,
the chambered nautilus
at the end of the block.

I, too, needy of art
in my middle age, discovered
my love. But, no slim needles
for me, no mini-circles
the size of a cat's eye,
no tissue-thin geometry
I can crush with my thumb.
I'm learning the letterpress,
that clanking flagship of the print shop,
that fossil of the book age.

Nine hundred pounds of metal
clatter in my garage. The back
of my truck swamps in foundry
type, and the names of the faces
roll from my tongue like gospel
hymns: Garamond, Helvetica, Century
Schoolbook, and Bembo. No sewing

box for me, no microscopic thread.
It took two friends and me
three hours and a hydraulic hoist
to raise and lower my press
from the bed of the red Toyota,
one iron foot clinging in a groove
each jerk. I will spend my old age

surrounded by wheels and cogs,
levers and treadles, feeding reams
of rainbow color to this Venus
flytrap which will spit them
back at me, imprinted
with words and lines, stories
my grandmother might have spoken
as she sat doing her lap work
in the exquisite evening light.

The Former Coach, Three Rows Up in the Stands, Cheers the Team

The last home game this season's halfway through.
I've watched them all. I've cursed the refs, thought best to pray.
Next year will be here sooner than you know.

You make each game the most important one, show
what you've mastered, flip your tricks out for display.
Commitments made, you force the play and follow through.

When I was coach, each error flared and glowed
in neon in my sleep. Scoreboards haunted me for days.
Next year will be here sooner than you know.

I let the losses tug, an undertow.
I had to charge the current, break away.
Commitments made, I had to learn the stroke and follow through.

It's true: I left this game with sorrow.
I'm in insurance now. Recruitment's still the crucial word, I'd say.
Next year will be here sooner than you know.

It's futile to predict how life will go.
The second half's already underway.
Commitments made, you force the play and follow through.
Next year will be here sooner than you know.

The Minister Takes a Back Road on her Way to Church

Notice how, along the back roads,
Queen Anne's Lace
breaks out in long-stemmed
constellations. They grow
unnoticed, so common
and so plentiful.

Watch how the raven rides on air.
We do not see how he finds
the way to use its lift
to arrow him home.
He is darkness making
his way
toward light.

See the placement of barns
and Holsteins, silo
bracing the shed.
Old fences giving in
to slope. Once red,
once white, they return
to the fabric
of trees.

A train rips along
beside me. What hymn
do I hear in its wheels?
Stay with me, Stay with me,
Stay with me, they say.

I pull the truck
to the side of the road,
watch the train with its cargo of wishes go on.

I step out onto gravel,
loose footing, lift off toward
the tangible comfort
of stars.

The Traveller Crosses Eleven States in Early February
or
West to East Haiku

Columbia Gorge:
salmon struggle up river,
I fight snow for home.

If these pines were words
and the deep snow a blank book,
my poem for you.

The sadness of late
evening shadows on snow:
a shaft through my heart.

Under a full moon
in Idaho my red truck
runs like Coyote.

Snow makes a beach of
Wyoming. Dunes dip. Wind plays.
Sand in my truck's teeth.

Mother-of-Pearl Moon
out for a night on the town.
Sunset becomes you.

South Dakota waits,
something's about to happen:
Sioux on the next ridge.

Sharp eagle eye moon
plumed in the sunset sky.
Blue light everywhere.

Into Wisconsin,
as many cows as snowflakes.
No two are the same?

Rush through Chicago:
Remember not to look back:
a pillar of salt.

Over my house, orange
moon lolls, smug as a pumpkin.
Snow starts to fall.

The Former Nun Confesses

It was a bad Friday this year,
though it never seemed good to me,
even back then. I was depressed
about Jesus all day. I kept thinking
how it must have been to be abandoned
like that, to have the one voice
he trusted disappear into memory.
Did he wonder if all this were his fault,
if somewhere along the way he'd forgotten
a crucial prayer or neglected to lay hands
on some unassuming head? Did he really believe
this could happen to him? I think of the blood,
the headgear of thorns, the vinegar sponge.
What could make a father that disposed
to give pain?

Wednesday, while I was out poking holes
in the moist earth, pushing the seeds
knuckle-deep, I recalled this
would have been his last normal day.
We know about Thursday, about Friday.
But what happened on Wednesday?
What did he choose those last hours? What
would I do my last day, today? Clean the house,
fold the clothes, walk the dog. Write letters.
Pay bills. Take my daughter to spend the night
at her best friend's. Could I not believe
there would be one more day, time
to see this garden flood
violet with bloom?

The Professor Maps Her After Hours Itinerary

Each night I leave home
and commute to the inner-city
of dreams. It's an easy ride
with only a few stops early on
when someone with a voice like wind chimes
calls on the phone for my son
or the gangster on the downstairs t.v.
machine guns his way into a bathroom.
Jolts, bright lights, a persistent bark
in the distance, then the train
of the story runs on. I never ask
questions or wonder why

I am riding a Greyhound Bus with a woman
I haven't seen since childhood. The rooms
look familiar, though I can't say
how and my dogs have gotten out
under the fence, again. How strange
this ocean plows through Kansas,
its beach sprouting umbrellas on a grey day.
But I've forgotten something
important which turns out to be
a suitcase full of purple
dresses I'll need for the bike trip
through the woods where I grew up in the kitchen
with five graduate students whose names
I can never remember in alphabetical order
because my friend Susan has appeared
for a surprise visit with the dry cleaning
in the middle of the worst snowstorm
I've ever seen though I'm barefoot
with my husband who keeps turning off
an alarm clock filled with flowers
on the dashboard of my truck

at roller coaster speed, we whiz
home with the dawn, tunneling through
the neon graffiti of my life
and I step out of the lavender sheets
(the radio plays something that's early Bach)
suffering from jet lag and coming down
with a terrible cold.

The Lover Takes a Letter from Her Mailbox

I hold it now, unopened.
Your words, four days old, start
to stir between the folds.

Which of us gives them life?
Do they breathe in the letter unread?
Unread, do they diminish to their thin bones?

Unopened, this letter
is power. It is lava cruising
toward the surprise of the century,

the wolf hungry and hurt.
It is the call to come,
the reason to go.

I can fold it, wear it
on my heart's pocket,
badge or bandage.

I can slip it among
these poems,
flattened between longing

and fear. I take it now
from its sealed lips.
It springs loose

like a cat,
like a whisper,
like last night's rain.

The English Teacher, in Mid-Life

Today my life scrawls out
before me in misspellings and red ink,
a paragraph with no topic sentence,
a term paper interesting
to no one at all. Surely
I who have lived so many years
with Hamlet and Ishmael,
Hester Prynne and Martha Quest
can escape this life
of other people's lives,
this constant ministry
of words. I stand before
my students, Moses with tablets
in a foreign tongue, the Ten Commandments
for an "A." But I am
no old-time prophet
nor precursor of the Divine.
I cannot heal their fragments,
rescue their dangling participles
from sin, resurrect their breathless
themes. I cannot give words
their autumn hues nor can I bring
the loon's cry to desert ears.
I can make no choir of the dumb.
Each day language fails me
more and more. There are no words
to explain how the Brontes wrote
what they wrote or why
Virginia Woolf waded out
to sea. How do I tell them
what made Thoreau
search out Walden Pond?
The page lies dead, the pencil
a remembrance of things
past, a dinosaur bone.

Something Grandpa stuck
behind his ear, something
broken and blunt.
The chains of paper
weigh more than chains of iron.
They rattle in my sleep.
Then, she comes to me, holding forth
like communion bread a piece
she has written. I receive it
and read the words mixing together,
yeast and flour. She, too, has a life
of secret snows and dreams deferred.
We have more in common
than she knows. We schedule
an appointment for this same time
next week.

The Artist Travels the Kansas Turnpike, Wichita to Topeka, on Valentine's Day

Like the lone cowboy in the western films of my childhood,
I ride into these Flint Hills, the false fronts
of spring rising both sides of the road. This is the month
that, last year, brought the big snow, but for two weeks
now we've worn no hats or gloves. A haze hangs over
these faded fields, the landscape on the verge
of birth. I am trailing a pick-up, yellow
as a lemon in the bright sunlight, and watch it roll
into the dips and valleys of this double highway,
a bouncing ball I am to follow and sing along with.
What comes to mind is *Amazing Grace*,
these plains remarkably empty and Biblically bare,
the Promised Land somewhere just out of sight.
The truck stays a good ways ahead, though I'm catching up,
and no cars appear in the oncoming lanes. I see
this whole countryside washed out, a sepia photograph
too long in the sun. I am stunned
by the brightness of that truck,
a Chevy Chieftain, the only splotch of color for miles,
emitting vibrations throughout the terrain. The black
and white cows plodding around the gray pond
burst into purple and pink, the water they drink
the blue-green snorkeler's bay. The magic truck
sails on, and the flinty fossil rock
blooms in heather, alfalfa, goldenrod,
and sweetgrass. Trees tingle into blossom,
redbud and lilac. Ahead the windmills spin
kaleidoscopic tops, the red-tailed hawks
fan out their peacock plumes. Suddenly
the scene rolls back to silent film,
technicolor vanishing fast, as the yellow truck
turns off the exit at Admire.

The Woman Speaks from Several Branches Up

Nash's mistress, Juliana Popjoy, cared for him until he died
and then, unhinged by grief, went to live in a tree.
Smithsonian, November 1984

No one visits anymore.
I don't know whether they don't like climbing
stairs or if the autumn in their hair
seems brittle as old bugs. I like it here.
My green rug, my frosted windows
in the early light. No screen interferes
with colors that fight for brilliance
at day's end. And the million sounds
of evening I hear because the town's no longer
near. What I have missed these many years
is clear. In this place I can
scan the sky for prophets' clues.
But, why bother? If war looms
I'll see the moon spoil like a bad fruit,
get the first word from the rain,
that old gossip in the attic,
that broken faucet. There's plenty here
to do. Don't come bringing loaves
and news. No cameras, please.
The trees won't smile. Nor will I.
Don't mention unfamiliar names.
I am who remains.

The Enchanter, Offering an Interview

The training of wizards is a very
difficult thing. Wizards have to spend
years standing in a chalk circle until
they can manage without it.

Jeanette Winterson

As a child, chalk was my talisman,
my rod, my wand. My small friends
carried dolls and bats, toy cars
and guns. I kept to chalk,
my fingers pale as ghosts,
dusty shadows on all I touched.
White—the lightest of all colors,
the closest kin of invisibility.
A white circle, every point the same
distance from the center, the ring
whose beginning is its end.
The dragon, tail in its mouth.

Inside the circle I learned
my space: the chemistry of the heart,
the geometry of limbs, the alchemy
of the mind.
The tides of my circle are called
by the moon. My circle,
the silver coin of costly knowledge.
For years I drew the circle
seven times each day,
an odd accessory, worn like an earring,
a belt. The circle
taught me perfection.
To others I was a perfect
stranger, to myself,
the perfect crime.

I would never be caught.
No pointed cap with stars
and crescents, no long gown
sweeping the stairs.

With chalk on my hands
I scale the rocks,
decipher the symbols posing
as mere words.
It's always the mundane,
you know, the inconspicuous
that transforms:
the magic bean, the pumpkin, the toad.
No fanfare, no glitz.

Now you will not see the circle,
nor the chalk, though you might notice
how sound often falls short
of my ears and rain refuses to come
too close.
I will never be struck by lightning.
I will never be cold.

I have uncoiled the circle.
It strings across years
like a tightrope, a zipper
on the fabric of time and space.
I unzip and slip through at will.
I have mastered my own space,
a grid where I hopscotch,
the most delicate sleight-of-foot,
my dusty stone never long
in any one square.

The Poet Speaks: The Early Years

I

I chart the world in what ways I know:
the land as compass, the magnetic pull
            of water and rock,
the needle's arm of a road leading

north to snows deeper than our childhood
            wounds, snows we can only imagine
as vast fields of ripe wheat, what is at the center
of our ancestral knowing, what we know,
            what is bread;

to the south, to the slow incantation of lives
still lived in tradition long gone,
            whose memory
clings like the scent of lilac, the intoxicating
perfume of loss, the lugubrious summer
night, something we cannot quite touch,
            something
whose shadow roams the back stairway
of speech;

to the east, whose cities forge a landscape,
            steel and glass, tower
and underground, the recitation of numbers
and daily litany, a garbled bid for a grasp
            at the sublime, figures
scattered like Biblical seed across concrete,
where, incredibly, language, our own
            language, rings foreign

and false; to the west where the desert
promises no more than it can offer, which is more
        than we allow,
where coyote and moon howl their collaborative
        magic, they, the givers
of shimmering gifts, the shamans who will lead
the route to the sacred mountain, placing
on the tips
        of our dry tongues,

the wafer-thin shards of pots shaped by hands
who knew the book of tales
        we can never know,
the circumambulation of gods
we can never acknowledge
        as our own.

II

The words of the philosophers, the revered texts,
their mirrors of the inner workings
        of the soul
are only that—words and mirrors, symbols
of the intangible and polished surfaces
that give back the smile we give
        for what we see as real,
props for those who practice sleight-of-hand,
or sleight-of-word, who say:
        Watch this!
and direct our eyes to see only what they mean
for us to see, one hand making the iridescent scarf
disappear into air
        while the other hand,
the one we do not watch, busies itself
with the strings.

III

To learn what is genuine, to allow the voice
            which is ours
to become ours, to permit ourselves
to go alone into the darkness with no match,
with only the stars overhead and perhaps,
            a lighted window,
in the distance where the road forks, beyond
reach, and to believe that the night sounds
around us are our own sounds:
a foot cracking a twig, a heart pounding
beneath fabric and bone, the jingle
of the jacket's clasp, and beyond that,
            the machinations of the forest—
a scampering of sharp claws, a footstep
walking in our footprint, the flicker

of eyes in the brush—which we write
            into the scenario
with our own pens, by our own power to project
            the unreal into real,
the act of breathing breath into the shape
of our fears, of making move the fingers
that finger our coats.

IV

The external world holds all we know
            and all we do not know:
the slant of the barn roof, the photosynthesis
of the greeny realm, the starling
tugging the worm from the spring mud,
the hillside repopulating itself after fire
            and human scorch.
Watch the progress of the sun
through the day's course,

75

        the resurrection
of the crescent to perfection, the weather
of natural interaction,
the incalculable metaphor
            of a season's revelation.

The Poet Speaks: The Later Years

Gone from home for as long
as I lived here, I hear
your voice on the phone for the first time
in years, giving directions to roads
I know by heart, telling me how
to find you in the countryside
so altered I'll be startled as Alice
at the bottom of the rabbit hole,
or Van Winkle yawning his way back
into town. It's spring, just spring,
in the Appalachians. As I drive
deeper into the valleys, sadness
cloisters me like a diaphanous veil.
It's the light, I think,
the way the late evening light offers
solace, for what losses
we can't even know, or the way
the light in the last hour
before dark entices us
into memory. This is the light
in your voice as it falls
on my ear. I am drawn to what
I took years leaving behind,
to the girl left hanging
on a low limb of the persimmon.
The light down this valley
reels me in like a fish.
I sound out the words on the signs,
names that fit like a shed skin.
I go toward the center of this
venerable grief, expectation
gathering now like faint stars.

IV. A Third Eye

Stars

Are they out there or not?

I asked myself, a kid
squat on the back stoop,
elbows on knees, chin in hands,
pale frog on a cement pad.

It was a close August night.

The whole family wandered
the house, the yard,
ghost-like, in the sticky air:
my mother in her milky-way
nightgown, my father
in cotton shorts, my brother
in whatever he wore
when he slipped into sleep.

I knew the light
from those stars meant
nothing, that the flickers
I watched might be long
burned out, no pulse there
at all.

Where I saw flame,
no match,
where I saw spark,
no flint.

From behind me, pushing
through darkness and heat,
my mother's voice

called my father,
Come to bed,
and I wondered,
by the time those syllables
lit up my ears,

did she still lean
in the doorway
or already lie in another room

lost in night's heaven,
night's mystery?

Making the Journey

for my cousin, Cindy

Daughters of sisters, we are the sisters
neither of us had, this recognition
coming late in life like the gift
of a grandmother's diary excavated
in the attic, or a lost ring plucked out
from the seams of the couch.

It was there all the time.

When we outgrew the brothers,
we, the weird ones in each pack,
grew toward each other: you moved
from the west coast to the desert,
I came from eastern mountains
to the plains. You crossed

more than miles to arrive, a decade ago,
on my front porch that night
with two pots and pans, granola,
and a vegetarian dog.

I hadn't seen you since you were twelve.
Now you were twenty-one.

Until you said my mother's name,
I didn't know you, though I suppose,
to you, I looked the same at thirty
as I had at twenty-one.

And then I saw your mother
in your grin. How unlike our mothers

we had both become.

Yet here we stand this morning in your kitchen,
you rummaging through the fridge
for things to send me on my way with:
fresh apple cider, cherry tomatoes
from your garden, pears picked out

at the market yesterday, expensive
chocolates from a wealthy friend.
I take the cider and pears, remembering
those early mornings in summer,
years ago, when, sleepy-eyed children
stuffed into the packed-up family Ford,
we watched our mothers in the ritual swap
of perishables, nourishment passing

hand to hand, sandwiches neat and tidy
in their waxed wrap, red thermos jugs chattering
with ice. How far removed we thought we were

from those women in pedal pushers and dresses,
we who nested loose-limbed among luggage
and pillows, how unquestioned
their grown-up lives, their waylaid dreams.
This ritual returns like a third eye,

though we have no one watching,
no dormant critics who will tell
this story in their own way.

A Sense of Place

my body moves with the land
it lives on
slow and rough and round
in the hills of West Virginia
it cradles the rivers that echo
the Indians: Kanawha, Elk,
Monongehelia, and marvels in the deep
mines: bituminous and anthracite
flattening to stillness, then wind
in the fields of Ohio and Kansas
finding routine, order
in the harvest of corn and wheat
simplicity of cattle and barn
I drift with the wood smoke, the smell
of hickory and morning fog,
westward, then eastward
my roots in my hand
in the new soil, the new
air, I heel them in
for a season, wait
then search for a place
where the earth is more porous
where roots can draw water
but again they will not take
I wish for rhododendron
against a backdrop of snow

at times I am close
to what I cannot reach:
my gloves seem to know that
they go on my hands,
that they should not turn up
in drawers with socks or hats
or underwear

the guitar's case is a perfect fit
and the flame of the candle burns quietly
in its pool of ginger wax
where to spend holidays
is becoming a problem, though my knowledge
of geography is constantly increasing

I can now name the capitals of
most of our fifty states
although it grows harder to recall
which is mine
I must try to remember my own name
write it down

Baptist Hymns

for Marcia, Marilyn, Nancy, Beth
Susan, and Eileen

They come to me at the oddest times,
tumbling out warm and electric
like the cotton socks and underwear
    A charge to keep I have, a God to glorify
when I let down the door of the dryer
or rolling in like a Friday night storm
as I stand looking across the lake.
    All hail the power of Jesus' name
In my Friday night writers' group—
a Baptist, an Evangelical United Bretheren,
two Methodists, an Episcopalian, a Catholic and a Jew,
all lapsed and relapsed—we are talking
about the houses we grew up in.
I mention the gospel music purring
inside the white plastic radio,
turned yellow and permanently tuned
to static, when someone across the room
breaks into *The Little Brown Church in the Vale,*
and before long we're all holding
hands and singing *Jesus Wants Me for a Sunbeam*
and *Bringing in the Sheaves.*
Except for our Catholic, who rises
to her feet, ceremonious and erect, and offers
Latin incantation that silences us all
in the middle of *Verse Two, Repeat Refrain.*
How mysterious those a capella
words, how seductive that ancient tongue.
This is what my mother, keeping watch
in the choir loft, was afraid I might hear.
Instead, I discovered the Pre-Raphaelite
poets and Matthew Arnold, though as I stand each year

before my class reciting *Dover Beach*, the sea
   I was sinking deep in sin, far from the peaceful shore
of those old songs may come crashing into the text:

It's Easter Sunday, I'm in grade three,
my new dress with its stiff crinolines
makes me bob like a buoy and I glance down
to the page of my hymn book, though I never
need to look at the words, and squeezed
between my tenor father and off-key grandmother,

I join my eager monotone voice
with those rising around me, feeling the refuge
of song, *the power in the blood,*
and love lifting me,
(even me).

What I Would Have Told You If I'd Called Home

Daddy, I'm in a motel in Junction City, Kansas.
I've put aside the work I brought: a novel
I've been trying to read for weeks, three unfinished
poems, and a complete set of papers from students
I've got to see next week. I've turned on the t.v.

It's October. The autumn color drowns in the grey drizzle
along I-70, but Cardinal red and Royal blue
blaze on the motel screen. It's the first game
of the World Series, 1985. They're calling it
the All-Missouri Series, one team perched on
the state's west end of the interstate, the other
on the east. Fans will drive the four hours back and forth
each way all week. I imagine that long, straight highway
dipping like a see-saw with their weight. Tonight
the Kansas City end hits bottom, folks flooding the stadium
in tides like these t.v. graphics.

I know you're watching in Florida, ceiling fan spinning
noiselessly overhead, herons perched in trees outside
by the boat dock. I remember how, back in those sweaty
childhood summers, we drove the asphalt, curling like wood
shavings, out of our mountains to Cincinnati to see the Reds.
Every August we went once. I couldn't tell you now
who played, but I do remember the air conditioned room
of the Fountain Square Hotel, the heart-squeezing rides
at Coney Island, the foot longs and champagne
sparkle of soft drinks. Then I grew up, left home,
haven't been to Cincinnati for years.

On t.v., the wife of the man who built Royals' Stadium
gets ready to throw out the game ball. She is dressed
for the opera, not the ball park, a flower
bigger than a baseball exploding on her chest. She holds

the ball, her hands cupped around it as if protecting
something breathing, something frail. Perhaps she feels
it has a life of its own. Her eyes steal toward her husband,
back to the stands, to the camera. The announcer instructs her
to toss the ball toward the pitcher, standing alone
in the foreground. As the ball arcs over the turf, I reach
for your box of popcorn, wanting to ask a dime
for the man in the greasy striped apron yelling,
Peanuts, Hot Roasted Peanuts!

Splitting Wood on Sunday

My mother would tell me this
is all wrong, this splitting wood
sunup to sundown. *This is God's day,*
she would say. *Do not work.*
But God doesn't work
two jobs, raise two kids, drive 300 miles
every week, have a roof that leaks,
a basement that floods, storm windows
to put up, and a wood box empty
with snow coming on. I think how
this wedge drives into elm like old grief: simple
pressure at first, then the wound, then the ripping
of fiber, popping of bark. Sometimes a clean
slice, the two halves of the apple plopping
either side of the knife. This is rare.
Consider the ragged lightning,
the punky stump.
More often the wood cracks, fissure random
as a fault line, the halves of the log
like Siamese twins, refusing to let go.
I remember my fork wound in countless strands
of spaghetti, the web of twine snarling everything
in the kitchen drawer. And my comb in
her uncombed hair.
If the wood is still green, the strings
braid to each other like licorice whips, the wedge
tentacled in. That's how it was
when she died, my heart
tangled in the sinews of her words.
I smack the netted wedge again, feeling
sledge bite steel, praying
for release.

Taking Down the Tree

on January 5th, everyone in the house
gone, I wrap the glass balls in pieces
of old socks as my mother taught me.
The tiny wooden chair, a private symbol
of grief, goes in the carton near Patrick's
glass cat and the red metal trikes and sleds
get parked in the last compartment.
When I unwrap the strands of lights,
spiraling like memories, I wind them
in neat wreaths, as my father taught me,
return them to their cellophane packs.
This tree was dead before its time.
The tiny knives slide under my nails,
attack my palms. I try to be gentle
with brittle branches, not snapping them
as I unclip the lamps, though I know
they are destined for mulch and flame.

From the tape deck, voices
of the Cincinnati Women's Choir,
Music in my Mother's House, fill the room.
I glance out the window at the new wind chimes,
green with tinsel stripes like candy canes,
frantic in the chaotic weather.
What did it sound like before this gift?
I wonder, and think how they take me back
to something I can't name, some place
where small, delicate chambers bump together
in a lost time, aiming a peculiar note
my way. *O Tannebaum, O Tannebaum,*
the chimes sing out. I see the choir,
a forest of voices in their green robes,
notes exploding among them
like colored lights.

Nightwork

Doing homework, often I was as perplexed as Alice in the Looking Glass.
First came arithmetic, the hardest, and making those fractions numbers
that were whole. While I grouched at my desk, my grandmother,
arms full of mending or rugs to shake out, would urge me to study
the problem once more, and then she would help. I would dream
about Saturday, going to Susan's, when word problems took no time.

At Elk Grade School I learned to spell, to tell time,
to measure in fathoms and furlongs, to count how many glasses
of milk I needed each week. On the playground, in my daydreams,
I was the boy who sank the winning basket, always the number
one man on the team. How I tried to be a boy. I had to study
hard to be the best girl in the class. I rarely saw my grandmother,

always there when I jumped off the bus, my quiet grandmother,
in her cotton house dress, turning her time into my time.
Thirty-five years distant, I think of her, a study
in patience, and remember the 1930's photo in a glass
frame on my desk. She wears her white Sunday hat. The number
of polka dots on her dress tests my mathematical skill. I dream,

sometimes, she's with us still, seem never to guess it's just a dream.
In these fragments, I discover, she often comes not as my grandmother,
but as a friend, someone I know well. Perhaps as my number
of years approaches hers and our ages pull closer in time
(she died, ten years older than I am now), we pass through the glass
walls of three generations, easy as apparitions, to be one. I study

her portrait that smiles self-consciously in the study
and think how our lives parallel in ways I could not dream
as a child. I want to squirm into that picture, slip through the glass,
appear beside her at the cabin door. *Grandmother,*
I would say in my most adult voice, *I have much more time
these days. There are some stories I need you to tell, a number*

of questions I need answers to fast. But all the numbers
I memorized, tables of distances, those charts and graphs I studied
for days, cannot help me travel across time.
My best chance for companionship still comes in dreams
where we hold spirited conversations at the kitchen sink, my grandmother
and I, doing the supper dishes, while the sun fingerpaints the glass

we look out through, where infinite numbers of stars will soon spark
                              the sky. I study
each word she gives me, adding, subtracting this time,
                              to prolong the dream:
a neighbor's glance catches my grandmother and me talking,
                              behind glass.

Leaving Adams Studio, MacDowell, 1989

Grey and wet outside, good weather
for blowing in the clouds of grief that come
with every loss. I've packed
my clothes, dirty jeans and sweats

in the big duffle, clean shirts
and socks smelling of sun-dried cotton
in the small. Next the books
and mail, and not until the last

moment, its presence in the room
a humming pregnancy, a miracle
of virgin birth, the typewriter.
Like mollusks, we abandon

our shells, grow into new ones
we can leave behind.
Before me, this one
kept a painter whose passion

sweeps across the walls,
whose prisms of color still wing
through the air. Before her,
a sculptor chiseled his vision

into fine woods. The surrounding
trees echo in this open room.
Shavings curled around his toes
like smoke, the light

igniting them. Myself,
I've filled the room with words,
those unruly beasties lurking
in the underbrush of thought,

and cat's eye marbles gnashing
their teeth in a rusty can. Some days
I found my words doused
in acrylic and oils, brightness

beaming up through the keys
like a lamp. Other days the words
were lumps, nouns needing
the chisel, whole lines exposing

themselves for the plane.
The old ghosts and I got on
superbly, their shapes
and color haunting

my black and white type.
I fancy their humor, the way
they turn a perfect square
tactile and fluid.

The fire's burned down, the north
light fades to ash. What ghost
of mine resides I can't surmise.
Perhaps a gentle snow

of letters will begin, a flurry
by dusk, accumulating
a random text. When the next
artist lumbers in, laden

with boxes and crates, easels
and paint, she may step
into a story forming
on the floor, only a minor

character at first.
Soon, she'll take the lead
as she designs her way
into the next few weeks.

Walking the City at Night

I would not do this at home.
This would be called taking risks,
taking chances, asking for it.
It is never defined until after
it happens.

I am walking a narrow sidewalk.
What lurks in the shadows
are old buildings. What lurks
in the old buildings depends
upon whom you ask. Or whether
you are a man
or a woman.

I step through the gridwork
of shadows drawn on the walk
by the streetlights. I hear
my own sandals flapping, the click
of high heels approaching, the ticking
of bicycle wheels whizzing by
in the street. I enter a tunnel
of trees. There are no fairies
in this forest, no magic mushrooms,
no princes testing their luck as toads.
If a strange man comes out of the bushes,
assume you have only one shot.

The lights of my building blink on
in the concrete slab ahead. They wrap
the tower like filmstrips or slides
illuminated from behind. A scene
is taking place in each window,
each frame. My window is blank,
as it should be. My scene
is taking place out here.
My scene is a woman walking
toward home in the dark.
This scene does not have to occur outdoors.

Late in the 4th Quarter

This time, your letter comes
by phone, and this time, it is you
squeezed tight by pain, not me.
Someone you love has left you now
for good. Always before you've been the master
of the sleight-of-hand, vanishing just before
the axe falls, or popping, like a rabbit
from a hat, into someone else's life,
or ducking out the back door
while the bride dresses upstairs.
But tonight, the private you
unbolts the lock and asks me in.

We used to talk like this ten years ago
on phone lines looped from the Ozarks
to the plains, you calling every Sunday,
me every Wednesday night. It's Sunday
now and the San Francisco 49ers have just scored
the winning touchdown in Superbowl XXIII,
with fifty-one seconds left on the clock,
when I pick up the receiver, surprised
to hear your voice. I'll remember this
in ten more years, just as I now remember
how I felt listening to the phone ring
inside your empty house or that I was reading
a poem by Adrienne Rich when you said
you wouldn't be home that night
I'd come to spend.

I hear you telling me she broke it off,
and grief leaks through even when you say
you're doing fine. If I could touch your letter
stringing out these words, the ink would run.
If I peer intently, I can still recognize the script.

Conversation at Beagle Gap

Up the trail, an easy climb
the ranger says, to a ridge
where the mountains tier around us
in choirs of blue mist, the wind,

in a minor key, tuning up for a song
native to these hills. Sunday morning,
and we're alone with whatever
gods we tote from childhood,

whatever gospels reach us
by way of sumac and squirrel.
This place feels new to you,
though old to me. You live here

now, these hills comfy as old shoes,
necessary as bread. I wonder
how I could have ever left.
As we hike the trail we're looking

back beyond these hills, beyond time,
beyond the complex narrative
of past and present selves.
Middle age has caught us both

off guard. You're on the brink
of buying your first house.
I remember when I could pack
all I owned in a VW, and still have room

for the dog. You touch my arm lightly,
point down among leaves.
A woolly worm slinks his way along
moss, a rusty stain crossing

the rug. *This is an omen,*
I say. *If he goes north, it means*
one thing, south something else.
But I can't remember the folklore,

have no idea which way is north.
I kneel down, let his soft body
squirm into my palm, pass over my hand.
He never breaks stride. When he's back

in the leaves, my hand tingles,
the phantom trundling of his thousand feet.
If I close my eyes, I swear
he's still there. I rise, and we go

on down the steep path through rocks
flecked with red iron and quartz,
black walnut and dogwood
itching to bloom. Our talk wanders

its own trail, the promise
of the next viewpoint guiding us on.
We are beginning to understand
what history means, how it is

to find ourselves living
in a time not our own. We stop
to look at an elm whose branches
seem wrenched into place,

a forced reunion of tree trunk and limb.
My mother, you say, *can't be trusted alone.*
Her eyesight and memory are both nearly
gone. You snap a twig from the sassafras.

We pause at the gully.
Among the bare trees we seem garish
and loud. I marvel at the rebirth
of this hillside, the buds some token

of faith, a testament of return. The moss
at my feet, the tenacity of green in a brown
season. Catching our breath, we will climb
to the next ridge, then descend.

Reunion

For Peggy Mucklo and Emily Kilby

> *To live in this world*
> *you must be able*
> *to do three things:*
> *to love what is mortal;*
> *to hold it*
> *against your bone knowing*
> *your own life depends on it,*
> *and when the time comes to let it go,*
> *to let it go.*
> —Mary Oliver

All encounters with the past,
like a knife, have two surfaces: the familiar
gone a little strange,
the strange casting the long shadow
that's familiar.

Here's a photo: a woman
at a dinner party making a toast,
her drink chiming against yours.
I wasn't there, you say. *I don't remember*
her at all. But there you are,
despite what you know,
leaving this fingerprint
on the glass.

We try to determine how the boy with eyes
blue as fire tongues
died that last year, and who

104

was with Augie when the train snowplowed
his car 3,000 feet down the tracks.
I was at the party,
waiting.

≈   ≈   ≈

I loved you then, but couldn't name
my need, a microscopic floater
in the blood which could expand,
pressing veins into arteries,
arteries against organs,
organs into skin
until filled
with the helium force
of desire, I stretched
beyond tolerance.

≈   ≈   ≈

Then, life was an interruption
from our revels, our mad hurtling
toward some black hole,
some place where, together,
we would spin through to that new
world, to a gravity all our own.
This was the '60s, anything
was possible.

Now we interrupt our lives, change
our schedules to travel to each other
along interstates, this reunion
a hiatus in the story, a moment
out of the flow.
It's like watching an old movie,
the sequel running at the same time.

On our way to the movie, the moon
marbles the blue-black sky
with her light, clouds rolling in
like grey waves, dark breakers
adrift in the night sky.
This sky is an ocean sky,
I say, remembering the Newport
summer when we each loved
the wrong person and the moon beat
against the sky like a white-knuckled fist.
It's not quite full tonight,
the heart's missing.

I asked someone at work this week
for the best song in the last thirty years.
Tracks of My Tears, she said, and Smokey Robinson
sounds the same from your tape deck as he did
on our old record player in the farmhouse
apartment where we worked toward degrees.
These days, one of us works to save
the auxillary verb, another to reinstate
the subjunctive, the third to educate
to the fact that *man* is not a generic term.

I take home one of the African violets
you brought for us both,
willing the fleshy leaves
to flourish, the purple flowers
to bloom.

Anonymous

My grandmother told me only
that living in the past was no good
and never mentioned my grandfather
drowned trying to save another man.

My mother read me stories from the Bible
and *A Child's Garden of Verses*,
happy stories, she said, because
life has enough sorrow

you don't need to add more.
Aunt Marie never said she was first
married to a handsome, luckless boy
killed during the war

until I found the photo
no one could explain.
And Aunt Phyllis neglected to say
she was desperate until my uncle

lay dying in the next room.
Silence was the haunted field
each walked home through
alone, afraid that to cry out

was to give away her position.
What they couldn't see
in the darkness, those shapes,
those movements they took for lost souls,

were more women like themselves,
women tiptoeing lightly
as the sounds of ghosts,
the whisper of frost.

What they couldn't hear
was a legion of secrets denied
speech like a dog denied water
after a long run.

A pack of women drinking
could be a dangerous thing,
a pride of females,
an ostentation of ladies.

One drop of the sweet liquid,
they'd want more. Now my cousin
tells me what happened to her
at sixteen and I tell her why

I've lived with the same friend
all these years. My friend tells me
how she knew, on the night
of her wedding, it was a mistake,

and her friend relates
that when her mother died,
she felt nothing
but joy. Gossip, some people

would say, idle tongues.
I tell you these stories
are your own.
You have taken them in

like a foster child.
I tell you a true story
is a strange thing.
It is a poem

missing
the final lines
and you are at your desk
already writing.